Reformations In Prayer

Pastor Steve Eden

DEDICATION

I would like to dedicate this book to my beautiful wife
Stacy and our three children: Noel, Caleb, and Joshua; for
always sticking by me through all of our ups and downs
together. We are greater together than each of our
individual parts. Each of you mean the world to me!

CONTENTS

CHAPTER 1:
THE AVIS APPROACH

When people talk about commitment to prayer, spiritual disciplines, and even the dreaded "New Year's resolution," many of us unfortunately hearken back to a variety of personal failures of the past. So let me say quickly, this book on prayer is not about the disciplines of: "trying harder," "doing better," "praying longer," or "doing more." I often refer to these as the "Avis Approach" to Christianity, based on their old slogan from the eighties, "Avis: We try harder!"

We have all tried different ways to be good Christians and to get better "results," but so often the feebleness and inconsistency of our human self-effort has led to weakened intimacy with God, burn out, and frustration. The truth is we don't need more self-effort in the body of Christ, we need more self-surrender. In other words, we need to yield to the internal Presence of God's Holy Spirit, which allows His strength and power to come forth; not ours.

There's nothing more deceptive than living your whole Christian life FOR God. He doesn't need you to live it *for* Him, He needs you to live it *from* Him; as your Source.

This is the "I am" principle. In other words, whatever you have need of, He is! You need love? God says, "I am" the love you need. You need salvation? God says, "I am" the salvation you need. You need forgiveness? God says, "I am" the forgiveness you need. You need peace? God says, "I am" the peace you need. He is THE total answer to your total need.

Zechariah 4:6 says, "Not by might, nor by power, but by My Spirit says the Lord…"

This is such a wonderful way of stating how our human self effort is not to be the cornerstone of our walk with God. He seeks the simplicity of His Presence and Spirit flowing through our willingness and dependence. He's not asking us to be the sharpest knife in the drawer, but He does ask that we be IN the drawer.

When you look at Moses, the deliverance of Israel was clearly not going to happen without two things: God supplying the ability and Moses supplying the availability. God was upset with Moses in Exodus chapter 4; not because Moses doubted he could deliver the nation but because he doubted God could deliver the nation THROUGH him!

The Lord clearly delights in our need of Him. I honestly believe our human inadequacy is one of our Heavenly Father's greatest assets when we allow it to teach us reliance upon Him.

Avoiding Self Reliance

Our independent successes after the flesh (our efforts, not His) so often do us more harm than good. We soon believe our own "hype" and ability, gravitating toward self-reliance while failing to recognize our desperate need to depend on God.

2 Chronicles 16:9 says, "For the eyes of the Lord run to and fro throughout the whole earth, to <u>show Himself strong</u> on behalf of those whose heart is loyal to Him."

Notice who is to be strong in this passage. <u>It is the Lord desiring to show Himself strong through us; not our trying to be strong for Him.</u>

It reminds me of 2 Corinthians 12:9 where Jesus tells Paul:

"My <u>grace</u> is sufficient for you, for My <u>strength</u> is made perfect in weakness."

Jesus describes His grace as "strength" here. And how is it manifested? In our weakness. In other words, what does Jesus strength flow seamlessly through? Human dependence, not human self reliance.

James 4:6 says, "God opposes the proud but gives grace to the humble."

Our self-effort and pride short circuit the Lord's grace (His strength and empowering presence) more than anything.

Paul goes on to say in the rest of 2 Corinthians 12:9:

"Therefore most gladly <u>I boast in my weakness</u>, that the power of Christ may rest upon me."

<u>This is a foreign concept in most churches today where an emphasis on self-effort typically trumps any acknowledgment of weakness or need of surrender.</u>

Victory Through Surrender

Any Christian action whether it is prayer, worship, witnessing, service, or giving is not the whipping up of your will; it is the surrender of your will to the Lordship of Jesus Christ who is in you. Christianity is not surrendering one time at an altar, it's a life of on-going surrender to Jesus in the present tense.

If a person should say, "Pastor Steve, how do I handle the fact that someone is spreading rumors about me at my workplace? What should I do?" I would invite them to pray, seek, meditate on, and even visualize how and what CHRIST wants to say to that person. Then simply allow the Lord to execute His desire **through** them. <u>We fare much better when we submit our bodies, minds, attitudes, and mouths to Christ rather than act independently of Him and pray He bless what we just did or said!</u>

We've tried to do a lot of things with our "self" through the years. Think of the slogans: Express yourself, better yourself, improve yourself. These have been used as often inside churches as outside of them! We've even had sermon titles like, "7 Steps To A Better You."

<u>God doesn't need a "better" you, He needs a surrendered you.</u> A surrendered you to Christ is the best 'you' there is! The world says if we surrender we lose, but in the Kingdom of God when we surrender we are victorious!

When you surrender your "self" to Christ, you do not become a slave, you become free, for you have just surrendered to the One for which you were made. You are no longer the center; Christ is, and all of His grace and strength are free to flow through you!

All Of Me

How many people through the years have
walked a church aisle in order to be free when
we should've simply walked the aisle to be HIS.
Are we not most free when we most belong to
Him and His loving care? His wisdom? His
guidance? His holiness?

How many have boastfully said, "I have the
Holy Spirit" without ever asking, "Does the
Holy Spirit have me?" It's like we stand at the
bank of the river of God and throw in a stick
that says "All my guilt," "All my shame," "All
my past," and never discover what He really
desires is for us to walk straight into the river
and say, "All of me."

Steve Eden

Chapter 2:

"Proper Alignment"

It was October of 2009, Stacy and I were pastoring where we pastor now, and all was well (I thought). Early one morning, the Lord asked me to get out an old, unused journal someone had given me because He desired to share His thoughts regarding prayer and more specifically my prayer methods.

He said He wanted to *redeem* prayer for "His purposes" because it had drifted too far towards the purposes of man. He mentioned His desire to specifically move *me* away from things He called, "self-centered prayer," "need based prayer," "crisis prayer," and "prayers rooted in unbelief."

Definitely intrigued, I began waking up early in anticipation of all the "secrets" Jesus was so willing to convey. Little did I know, over those next few weeks, He would drastically change how I viewed prayer and completely transform our relationship. <u>Basically, He introduced me to an outlook on prayer that was centered on Him instead of centered on me.</u>

The First Reformation

The first thing the Lord said to me was, "Steve, you need to start using prayer to align yourself with Me and My purposes instead of always trying to align Me with yours." I was stunned.

How could I even know God's plan if I wasn't getting it from Him? Unfortunately, instead of allowing Him to tell me what He wanted, most of my prayer time was just *me* telling *Him* what I wanted.

I suppose I just assumed the plans I was praying and asking Him to "get in on" for many years were the plans He desired. This was of course until He said, "Steve, I like your plans, but My plans are a lot better."

Talk about an "aha" moment! I thought, "You are so right Lord. I'm quite sure Your plans are better than mine. Please forgive me of my ignorance and presumption."

While there are times to let God know what we are thinking; more often than not, we need to take time to know what He's thinking.

Suddenly I realized my plans were definitely much too small. They were limited by my own capacity, ability, and resource. I'm convinced now that if we have a plan that we can do, it's not from God! He's going to draft plans that are impossible without His help.

While my plans typically only involved me, the Lord began showing me His plan involves extending His Spiritual and Everlasting Kingdom throughout the whole world! Mercifully, He even wanted me to be part of it.

I was immediately sold! As a pastor, imagine the burden that was lifted off me because I no longer had to come up with my own plan, He had one! Now I could utilize prayer to know His will instead of telling Him mine.

He let me know how He desired to get His Spirit inside every human heart that would receive Him. He spoke of His loving, redemptive rule made so perfectly for our inner man.

He revealed how He came into the world not to condemn humanity but that humanity through Him would be saved and restored. This opened my eyes to a whole new perspective. <u>The world didn't look nearly as intimidating for I was aligning myself with the God of the universe and His plan; a plan that had cosmic backing and unlimited resource.</u> This was a grand plan that I wanted in on!

The Precedence of Alignment With God

I once heard it said, "Jesus is perfect theology," so with that, let's look at one of His prayers in the Gospel of Matthew.

Matthew 26:39 says, *"He went a little farther and fell on His face, and prayed, saying, "O My Father, if it is possible, let this cup pass from Me; nevertheless, <u>not as I will, but as You will.</u>"*

Here Jesus uses prayer to synchronize Himself with the Father's will & purpose. He often said He would only do what the Father was asking and showing Him to do. He was submitted at all times; always trusting in His Father.

Jesus consistently used prayer to align Himself with the Father's purposes. You will not find Jesus praying "me first," self absorbed prayers anywhere. You won't find: "Oh Father, please bless Me." "Father, please fund My ministry, I'm lacking resources." Jesus did not pray self-centered prayers.

The truth is anything that leaves you at the center will wind up off center, and that includes prayer. If the only prayers you pray are about you and for you, you're missing the incredible blessing of being God-centered and others minded. The job of being the center is already taken and it belongs to God!

You can insert any Christian activity in there whether it's praying, serving, witnessing, or giving; but if you're only doing it so you can get something for yourself, I advise you to re-consider it.

Let your motives be pure and uncluttered with self-centered attitudes that say, "I'm going to pray so I can get this;" "I'm going to evangelize so I can get this;" "I'm going to get married so I can get this;" "I'm going to minister so I can get this." These statements reek of immature, baby Christianity that is centered on one's self.

As we mature in Christ, our prayers and our motives should evolve deeper and deeper into a posture of Christ-likeness, intimacy, selflessness, and a desire to share all we *already have from God* with others.

Free From Pressure

Now, especially for any leaders and pastors; if you come up with your own plans and purposes, guess who's going to feel the pressure to fund them? You will. Guess who's going to feel the pressure to make them happen? You will. Guess who is going to burn out? You will!

I share with pastors all the time - - "It really works better if you take on Jesus' vision for the local church. Resist the temptation to come up with your own plans and then ask Him to bless what you're doing. Always keep in mind that HIS vision is a vision with cosmic backing that is already blessed and fully funded!"

You're going to take on a lot of pressure as a church leader if you have the responsibility of coming up with and then carrying out your own plans and ideas FOR Jesus. Instead, seek first the Kingdom of God and His righteousness, knowing all your lesser needs are guaranteed.

<u>Have you ever noticed in Matthew 6:25-33 how Jesus talked as if God was real and could actually be trusted?</u>

In Matthew 6:25-26 Jesus says, "Therefore I say to you, do not worry about your life, what you will eat or what you will drink; nor about your body, what you will put on. Is not life more than food and the body more than clothing? 26 Look at the birds of the air, for they neither sow nor reap nor gather into barns; yet your heavenly Father feeds them. <u>Are you not of more value than they?</u>"

Jesus went on to say, "Consider the lilies," and

"If God so clothes the grass, will He not clothe you?" He's basically saying, "What are you guys worried about? Don't you know how much you matter to your Heavenly Father?"

The answer is truly they did not know their value and that led to the root of their insecurities; yet you and I have the cross and the revelation of our Father's goodness through Christ. We have infallible proof of God's love for us!

We must be careful that our prayers are not rooted in doubt, worry, and in fear that we have to somehow cause our Father to notice, value, and care for us; because He already does!

My advice for any believer, not just leaders and pastors, is to know the Father's heart and get in on the Father's plan; knowing that all these other things we so often worry about will be added unto us.

The Cheerful Giver's Box

Trusting in the Father's goodness and relying on His plan is how Grace Church ended up with a "Cheerful Givers Box" at the back of the church. <u>Believe it or not, in 16 years of ministry we have never passed an offering plate in a service.</u> We do not beg people for money. We do not misuse Scripture and appeal to their flesh and greed to get them to give. We simply by faith trust God to provide for *HIS vision*. We know that He is revealing to His people the needs that arise. He does, as the greatest giver of all time, live inside every born again believer! He is not dead, but very much alive in the present tense today.

Honestly, if it's our Father's will, it's our Father's bill. The way I see it, if there is no provision coming into the church, then maybe the Father wants to send all of us to be part of His Kingdom work elsewhere. We are okay with that.

We understand that our identity, purpose, and value are not all tied up in what we DO as members of Grace Church. Our identity, purpose, and value come from who we are, whose we are, and both our corporate and personal intimacy with Christ.

Married To Jesus

The enemy has sold us a tremendous bill of goods in the body of Christ through the years. He has used many well meaning leaders to lure us into living life *for* God instead of *from* God. We end up whipping up our will, trying to work the Bible just right; or attempting new formulas to merit His love, attention, and provision.

This doesn't really compute because the Bible is clear that once we are born again, we are "married" to the Lord. It even says in 1 Corinthians 6:17 that we are "one spirit" with Christ, and in Ephesians 5:30 that we are "flesh of His flesh and bone of His bone."

<u>What earthly husband tells his wife, "Listen, I know we're married; I know you have my last name and we're technically one flesh, but you'll have to work for all my provision, protection, and anything else you want me to do for you."</u>

No! Once you're married, all that's his is hers and all that's hers is his. How much more as Jesus bride will we be taken care of!

We often act as if Jesus' love, provision, protection, and forgiveness are "sold separately!"

Imagine receiving Jesus at salvation, deeply present in your heart; but then thinking His love, provision, protection, and forgiveness are not included! The Lord broke me of that old thinking when he said, "Steve, I am both with you and in you. What did you not get when you got Me? Stop working for things that are already yours."

Steve Eden

Chapter 3:

"Learning To Receive"

The next reformation the Lord gave me was in learning to receive. He said, "Steve, I want to teach you how to receive in prayer. If you focus on receiving as much as you do on producing, you will bear more fruit than you ever thought possible."

It was around this same time, I read a statement from the late great missionary E. Stanley Jones that completely confirmed what the Lord was saying to me. Doctor Jones quote was, "Receptivity precedes productivity."

Receiving Is The First Law of Life

What was the first thing Adam did in the garden? He received the breath of God. What is the first thing a baby does once it is born? Receive air into its lungs. This is because we as humans can only give out to the degree we have first received!

Another good example of this principle comes from seed and soil. When a seed goes into the ground, it must first receive the nutrients of the soil, the water, and the sunlight before it will ever flower.

A woman has to first receive the seed of her husband before she can produce children after his own kind. In the same way, what must we do first to bear fruit after our husband Jesus' kind? Receive. As we do, it will produce! Good seed plus good soil always equals good fruit.

In John 15:4-5 Jesus says, "4 Abide in Me, and I in you. <u>As the branch cannot bear fruit of itself, unless it abides in the vine, neither can you, unless you abide in Me</u>. 5 I am the vine, you are the branches. He who abides in Me, and I in him, bears much fruit; for without Me you can do <u>nothing</u>."

You can do a doctrinal Greek study on the word 'nothing' in John 15:5, but I will save you the trouble; it literally means, 'nothing.' For years I always thought Jesus command in this passage was to go bear fruit and yet no matter how many times you read it, the command is for us to simply "abide."

Living By Supply

Once a branch is connected and receiving, it has done all that's required; now it is up to the Vine to supply what is necessary for fruit to be produced and revealed through the branch.

In order to be a fruitful branch, we simply abide in and receive from Christ. Let's use love as an example. What if we did not 'try harder' to love Christ, but we simply yielded to the love that He has for us first? What if we quit trying to earn it and actually lived as though we had it?

Once we yield to the love that He has for us, (take it in, drink it, accept it, dance with it, fellowship with it, participate with it); His love will come flowing out of us and we won't be able to stop it!

If we walk in unbelief, which would be *trying* to get Christ to love us, then we have already put our faith in a lie. The lie being we have to DO something to get Christ to supply His love. My question is how many good deeds do we have to do to finally justify in our minds, "Jesus *has* to love me now."

<u>Remember, the moment you set out to get something, you just told yourself you don't have something.</u> And if you are trying to get something that God says is already yours (like His unfailing, never-ending love), you are in unbelief my friend.

It is so much easier and restful to give away something you've actually received. It is beyond difficult to produce something you do not have or are still in the process of earning. Imagine the impact if Christians quit living like they're earning God's love and began living like they already have it!

1 John 4:19 says, "We love because He first loved us."

So who loves first? He does. Yet how many

people in the body of Christ; everyday, love God SO He will love them instead of walking in the reality He already does?

In John 13:34, Jesus instructs us to love others "just like I love you." This reveals the reality that Christ wants to be our Source for all things! You need love? He loves you first. You need joy? He supplies it. You need peace? He has it in bunches! Like any good husband, Jesus leads us by what He supplies TO us not by what He demands FROM us!

This is the essence of John 15:4-5. If we are short on loving others, we don't try harder; we simply understand that we are short on believing/receiving/accepting the depth of Christ's love for us. Show me someone who struggles loving others and I'll show you someone who struggles receiving and submitting to Christ's love for them.

Romans 5:5 says, "Now hope does not disappoint, because the love of God has been poured out in our hearts by the Holy Spirit who was given to us."

27

Notice "the love <u>OF GOD</u>" has been poured into your heart by the Holy Spirit. <u>You may find this hard to believe, but Jesus Christ actually sources you from His Spirit the love He wants you to love God with!</u> This is a far better, more genuine, pure love than any human 'love' that we ourselves could conjure up in our own might and power.

<u>Every creation must live in the dimension that sources it. Fish must live in water because water supplies life to fish. A plant must live in soil because the soil supplies life to plants. Every human being must walk and abide in the Spirit because the Spirit of God is life to us.</u>

I was visiting with a lady recently who was struggling with unforgiveness toward another person. She was working hard at forgiving but to no avail.

I told her she had the cart before the horse and to start by receiving God's forgiveness for her mistakes first. <u>I said, "If you don't receive God's forgiveness first, you'll be unable to give away something you don't have."</u>

She marveled at that, saying she had never heard that in her life! She knew it was right and admitted she had always struggled with receiving God's forgiveness. She made the decision to humble herself and totally accept Christ's cleansing of her sins past, present, and future; and of course forgiveness happened *in* her and then *through* her supernaturally. It truly was powerful! She demonstrated how forgiveness heals two ways: When you get it, and when you give it!

Ministry Comes From Intimacy

During this time in my life, the Lord mentioned something that really stunned me. He said, "Steve, ministry born out of intimacy is a beautiful thing, but ministry *instead* of intimacy is idolatry."

I clearly had been trying to be more disciplined and focused on producing in ministry than I was on receiving. He said, "Steve, if you want to be disciplined in an area, be disciplined in receiving and spending intimate time with Me."

It's one thing to work for the Lord; it's life and peace when you work *from* Him, but it takes humility; something we've sorely lacked in the body of Christ. It also takes dependence; something else we've sorely lacked in the body of Christ. If we did a nation-wide survey and asked people for one word that describes the body of Christ in America, I don't think either the words "humble" or "dependent" are what we would hear.

That is unfortunate because God says in 1 Peter 5 and in James 4 that He opposes the proud but gives grace (His empowering Presence) to the humble. <u>We need to understand that maturity is not our becoming more independent from God but rather our becoming more and more utterly dependent.</u>

Blessed Are The Receptive

In Matthew 5:3 (New English Bible) Jesus said, "How blessed are they who know their need of God, all of heaven belongs to them."

Jesus is bringing the best news a hopeless/sinful human being could ever hear: The condition to have a relationship with God is not spiritual abundance but spiritual bankruptcy! It is not our hands full of our own merits, bill of rights, provisions, or religious efforts, but it is two open and empty hands!

The reason you have people sit in church their whole life and never move forward or mature is because they were never told the qualification for walking with God is receptivity.

Imagine, relationship with God no longer being defined by our eagerness to *achieve for God* but rather our humble willingness to *receive from God.*

Jesus says "All of heaven's resources – His forgiveness, love, and provision – are not for the most deserving, but for the most receptive." We see again the picture of our dependence as branches on the One True Vine.

How can we expect to produce and manifest holiness if it's not coming from the Holy One? Is it not fair to say true holiness comes from the Vine, not the branch? True Godly Holiness does not come *from* you, it comes *through* you.

If you're not careful, westernized Christianity will try to cause you to become an independent, self-sustaining branch. There – is – no – such – thing as an independent, self-sustaining branch! Be leery of taking all your Bible tools, all your prayer tools, and all your education and trying to do your best FOR Jesus.

Let me share with you a testimony. I received this letter from a 15 year old girl in our church:

"Pastor Steve, I have had pain in my lower back for the last month and I have prayed for God to fix it. I went to church last Sunday in serious pain. During prayer time, I put my head down and closed my eyes and stood there deciding, "I'm going to give this healing thing one last shot." I thought instead of asking and begging God to please heal me as I had done before, I would do what you said that morning and just "receive" the healing that was already mine through my relationship with Christ. As I was receiving, the pain first moved from my lower back to the middle area of my back. Then I just received more and more and the pain moved from the middle of my back to my shoulders.

Then the pain went up out of my shoulders and was gone! To this day, I do not have any kind of back pain and for that, I praise God."

Her testimony reveals what Jesus said is true: How blessed are the receptive! All of heaven belongs to those poor enough to receive and acknowledge their need of God.

Steve Eden

Chapter 4:

"Learning to Listen"

The next reformation the Lord shared with me was, "Steve, I have some wonderful things to say *to* you and *about* you, but you rarely give Me time to speak."

I thought to myself, "Why wouldn't prayer be TWO-WAY dialogue?" After all, if you are the only one talking in a relationship, chances are you aren't going to get to know the other person very well. And here I am doing all the talking to Someone who already knows me better than I know myself!

In John 17:3 Jesus said, "And this is eternal life, that they may <u>know You</u>, the only true God, and Jesus Christ whom You have sent."

Steve Eden

Jesus says the crux of Christianity is *knowing* He and God the Father, and yet wisdom says it's going to be hard to do that if we don't take time to listen to Them speak.

The Lord said, "Steve, you must utilize prayer to know Me, to listen to My heart, and to know My voice." 1 Samuel 3:9 became one of the cornerstones of my early morning prayer time. It says "Speak Lord, for your servant is listening." Notice, it does not say, "Listen Lord, for your servant is speaking."

Our Source For Truth

In John 10:27 Jesus said, "My sheep hear my voice, I know them, and they follow Me."

One of the many reasons it is important to listen to and know the Lord's voice is so He can be our source for truth. Pause for a moment and think, "Who is the source of information I use to determine what is true about me, about God, and about others?"

There are many voices out there trying to deceive you about who you really are, what you

36

really have, and what Christ can do through you. It is essential that you know the Good Shepherd's voice and are reminded that the truest thing about you is what He says about you, not what everyone else says!

What might His voice of truth do for our broken self-esteem and approval addictions? It is beyond difficult for the enemy to conquer a heart with his lies that's already conquered with God's truth! <u>Most Christians are not bound by satan but by assigning too much value to wrong voices and opinions.</u>

I find it so revealing in Genesis when God asked Adam, "Who TOLD you that you were naked?" In other words, who have you been listening to Adam because I never told you that! In the same way, I would ask you: Who told *you* that you were no good? Who told *you* that you weren't forgiven of your past? Who told *you* that you weren't clean and close to God? I am certain it wasn't your Good Shepherd.

Oh how we are transformed when we dare to believe all God says about us no matter how good it is!!

Psalm 107:20 says, "He sent His Word and healed them."

<u>The voice of the Spirit and God's Word are healing and life to you</u>. Why? Because you and God's Word are affinities. In other words, you were made for each other.

Jesus said in John 6:63, "My words are spirit and they are life."

When a flower turns its gaze to the sun, it opens with life. This is because the flower and sunlight are compatible; even "made for each other." In the same way, when a human being turns his or her gaze to the Light of God's Word, they open with life just like the flower. This occurs because we are compatible with the voice of the Spirit and God's Word.

The Challenge of Listening

The great author Henry Nouwen once wrote: "When I go to prayer, I realize, although I have a tendency to say many things to God, the real work in prayer is to become silent and listen to the voice that says good things about me."

That is the real work of prayer – silence and listening.

Psalm 85:8 says, "I will hear what God the Lord will speak, for He will speak peace to His people and to His saints…"

<u>Why is there such a lack of peace in the body of Christ today? Because we don't take time to listen to the voice of the one that speaks peace to His people.</u>

I don't know if most Christians think God doesn't want to talk to us "lowly people," or He chooses only to speak to the "elect select," but it is your birthright as a child of God to hear God's voice. It is not just some special privilege that church elders, deacons, or TV preachers have.

One of the greatest gifts we can give the Spirit of God is listening. We all want to bless Him and honor Him right? Well, sincere listening is a way we can do that. As you listen with your spirit to His Holy Spirit, you may be surprised at how an on-going knowledge of the Truth sets you free from lie based thinking.

Steve Eden

Chapter 5:

"Christ Is Deeply Present Within"

The fourth reformation the Lord gave was, "Steve, you pray as if I'm way off in outer space somewhere, separate from you. You will hear My voice so much better and experience much greater intimacy when you see I am deeply present within you."

Galatians 2:20 says, "I have been crucified with Christ; it is no longer I who live, but Christ lives in me..."

I had heard this passage before, but I guess I just never really considered it's depth. I began meditating on the reality of what Paul wrote: "Christ lives IN me... Christ lives IN me...."

Too often as Christians, we think we are these independent, autonomous (self-governing) beings down here on planet Earth doing our best for God. That's why so many struggle to hear God's voice because they are waiting to hear an actual audible voice flying down from Heaven somewhere. How often does that happen?

The Scriptures are very clear; once you're born again, Jesus Christ's very Spirit is intimately present within so we can experience true closeness and intimacy with Him as well as become more familiar with His voice.

Colossians 1:27 says, "To them God willed to make known what are the riches of the glory of this mystery among the Gentiles: <u>which is Christ in you, the hope of glory</u>."

1 Corinthians 6:17 says, "He who is joined to the Lord is ONE spirit with Him."

Even though God <u>IS</u> present everywhere, what a revelation that He, as the everlasting Father, Creator of the Universe dwells inside of us!

His indwelling is of necessity because we can never be like Him or reflect Him through mere human imitation. We simply cannot be like God apart from God.

God knows this of course; therefore, He gave us the inward gift of Christ at salvation. This is the only way His Life and Spirit could be manifested through His spiritual sons and daughters. The Spirit of God sows, our soul receives, that the body may reveal the Life of Christ within.

John 1:12 says, "To as many as received Him, to them He gave the power to become children of God."

If you thought you got born again and were made God's child because you signed a card and joined a church, you are mistaken. A church nor a signature can make a child of God. Only Father God, who is Spirit (John 4:24), can produce spiritual sons and daughters after His own kind. He moved inside of you so you could know Him intimately and so He could make Himself known to others through you.

43

Separation Theology

The Lord asked me to stop practicing "separation theology." He said, "Steve, My Word says I am ever present with you and in You. I am there to make good on my promises: "I'll never leave you nor forsake you," "I'm a friend that sticks closer than a brother," and "I'll be with you always, even until the end of the age."

In John 14:16-18 Jesus said, "16 And I will pray the Father, and He will give you another Helper, <u>that He may abide with you forever</u>-- 17 the Spirit of truth, whom the world cannot <u>receive</u>, because it neither sees Him nor knows Him; but you know Him, for He dwells with you <u>and will be in you</u>. 18 I will not leave you orphans; <u>I will come to you</u>."

In verse 16 Jesus clearly says once His Spirit moves inside you, He will abide with you forever! That is a much better condition and duration than, "I will be with you until you mess up." This means you actually have some security in your relationship with Him. You can now know He is going to be faithful to you and to your development until the end! Plants do not grow very well when they are constantly uprooted, do they? It is when they are secure in their soil that they really begin to thrive!

Now that we understand that Christ is present with us and in us, we will be able to hear His voice so much better. I know it completely changed my ability to hear!

Now is the time to set our hearts to know Him via His internal Presence. It is time we set our hearts to walk close and intimate with Him. It is time we yield ourselves, our minds, and our bodies completely to Him allowing Him to live and love through us from the inside out!

Steve Eden

Chapter 6:
"Our Highest Good"

Another reformation the Lord revealed was, "Steve, why do you use prayer to try and convince me what you think your highest good is? I AM your highest good."

How convicted and humbled I felt-- like I would know *better* than my Heavenly Father what I needed each day. And how could I possibly think material things could satisfy my inner longings like He could?

If we aren't careful, we can find ourselves uttering prayers like, "Oh God, I've got to have *this* to be happy." "God, you know *this* will fulfill me." "God, I'm calling on the prayer team so I can get what I *have* to have."

These just do not make sense when you consider material things can never satisfy us; yet, that's how I prayed for years!

It was during this conversation with the Lord the light came on that He was actually for my family and me. My Heavenly Father had no interest in withholding things we needed. I began to trust Him when I prayed, thanking Him for His love, provision, and protection; instead of begging Him for stuff I thought would make us happy.

Isn't it interesting how the Lord shifted me from fear-based prayer to faith-based? I literally began trusting in His goodness. It really hit me that I was His child and it wasn't all up to me to cause Him to be good to my family and me. I think I had finally entered a place of rest in prayer.

In Matthew 6:6-8 (Message Bible), Jesus says the following regarding prayer:

"Here's what I want you to do: Find a quiet, secluded place so you won't be tempted to role-play before God. Just be there as simply

and honestly as you can manage. The focus will shift from you to God, and you will begin to sense his grace. 7 The world is full of so-called prayer warriors who are prayer-ignorant. They're full of formulas and programs and advice, peddling techniques for getting you what you want from God. 8 <u>Don't fall for that nonsense. This is your Father you are dealing with, and He knows better than you what you need.</u>"

Imagine that, according to verse 8 our Heavenly Father actually _knows_ what we have need of even before we ask. This one statement cut down on my "asking time" in prayer considerably!!

God Is Good; Isn't He?

Notice in Matthew 6:7 Jesus says the world is full of so-called prayer experts who are actually prayer ignorant. They're full of formulas, programs, and advice designed to get YOU what YOU want from God. In verse 8 of this translation, Jesus calls such prayers "nonsense."

How many times though have we put all our efforts into formulas, praying 'right', and 'having enough faith' to try and cause God to be good to us? Do we really know the heart and love of our Father when we act like He is a reluctant giver?

First of all, God doesn't work for us. He is not our cosmic errand boy waiting on our obedience to send Him scurrying to bring us rewards. Secondly, and perhaps more importantly HE IS GENEROUS & GOOD!

Psalm 34:8 says, "Taste and see the Lord is good."

If we are honest, when blessings, provision, and protection come our way, it is not because we're so good, it's because He's so good! The moment we start thinking it is our works, techniques, or formulas that are causing God to be good to us, we are doubting His inherent goodness as our Father. We are also creating "debt" in our minds that our Father "owes" us. I believe it is dangerous any time that we are demanding God to, *"give us what we deserve."*

Romans 4:4-5 says, "Now to him who works, the wages are not counted as grace but as debt. 5 But to him who does not work but believes on Him who justifies the ungodly, his faith is accounted for righteousness."

This verse reveals that if we are "working for God," then we start believing He 'owes' us a payoff. Honestly though, what are we working for? Is it not written that we have been given, "all things that pertain to life and Godliness?" We should never try to get by behavior what God has already freely given us in Christ. This comes from the lie God is somehow holding out on us.

How can we live from a place of lack when He's given us His Spirit, His Word, His Kingdom, and His Son? How can we live from a place of need when all of Heaven belongs to us? We are his children! We are joint heirs with Jesus! Everything He has, we have! We must lose our poverty mentality and live from ALL our Father has already made available to us through Jesus Christ!

<u>Faith is living from what God's grace *has* supplied, not us doing religious things to convince Him to supply it! Your faith cannot appropriate what God's grace has not provided.</u> God's grace ***has*** provided things like salvation, healing, and forgiveness; however, things like cadillacs, cash, and condos I'm not so sure.

Satisfied In God

I want to be so satisfied in God, (so Psalm 23:1 the Lord is my Shepherd and I shall not want) satisfied, He has to tell me when I actually have need of something.

Let's go back to the beginning. In the garden of Eden, Adam was doing perfectly fine, he was in love with God and lacked for nothing. Adam wasn't lonely. He didn't say, "God why is there no dating service here on planet earth? How come there's no websites I can go to for single ladies?" He wasn't feeling incomplete and whining about it to God in prayer.

Adam was so satisfied and content in God, the Lord had to *tell him* what he had need of. God is who said, "It is not good for you to be alone."

In other words, "Here is a need you have Adam; let Me find you a helpmate." That level of trust and contentment is a great place to be in our Christian walk.

A Swift Kick

I felt like God had kicked me square in the behind when He asked, <u>"Steve, why do you and so many pastors teach people to use prayer to get *things* when they are too great a creation to be satisfied by things?"</u>

This one cut deep. Could I have been leading people into a model of prayer that ultimately wouldn't even satisfy the longing in their soul? He added, "Teach them to utilize prayer to know Me first, to synchronize themselves with Me. Only I can satisfy the human heart."

I repented immediately, for truly Christ is to us what a vine is to a branch, gasoline is to a car, and oil is to a lamp – Life!

Colossians 1:16-17 says, "We are made by Him and FOR Him. 17 And through Him all things are held together."

Without finding Christ and His love and acceptance, we humans tend to fall apart. Substitutes and imitations won't do. <u>Jesus Christ has cornered the market on human fulfillment; yet how many of us fall for the prayer "experts" peddling their techniques so we can get things?</u>

Peter in Matthew 19:27, says, "Lord, we've left all to follow you. What do we get?"

Wow! I am so glad we never say or think that, right?

We really must be careful of saying, "Lord, I performed well today. What do I get?" "Lord, I prayed hard today. What do I get?" "Lord, I didn't sin today. What do I get?" "Lord, I quoted scripture today. What do I get?"

If you're doing any of these things with your heart set on "getting," you may have missed the reality that only Jesus satisfies! Not only that, but you may miss the blessing of giving from a pure heart and participating with God's divine nature to help others. I really believe when we do as the Lord instructs, the payoff is in our person a lot more than some 'check in the mail.'

Now, there is a balance. It is totally acceptable for you to make your requests known to God; that's in scripture. But making your requests known to God must not be the only time nor the only reason you talk to God. I also understand the principle of sowing and reaping is still in effect, but the Bible also says, "If we sow to our own flesh, we will reap of the flesh (and it's motives) corruption."

"Father Make Me"

I want to close this chapter with a wonderful principle that comes from Luke 15 and the parable of the prodigal son. When the wayward son prayed (paraphrasing), "Father *give me*; give me my money, give me my share of the estate," the end result was he ended up hungry and willing to eat scraps in a pig pen saying, "I perish here with hunger."

After coming to his senses that living for yourself is not all it's cracked up to be; on his way home he changed his prayer to, "Father *make me* as one of your hired servants." The end result of this prayer was far from any pig pen as he received much more than he asked for. His father brought out the fatted calf, the robe, the sandals, and the ring!

What made the difference? I believe it is simply the intent of his heart. His prayer, "Father make me" was a prayer of humility, vulnerability, and submission. His prayer, "Father give me" was a prayer of entitlement and self indulgence.

Have we all not discovered the principle at work here? When we set out to please and fulfill ourselves, we are going to find lack and no lasting fulfillment. Yet when we place ourselves fully yielded into our Father's guiding hands, we end up triumphantly blessed!

Chapter 7:

"Father Use Me"

The last reformation the Lord shared with me was, "Steve, never be afraid to put action behind prayer. In many instances, I will likely want to *use you* to bring some of the answers."

In all my years of ministry, I never once had considered the thought God might want to use me to answer some of the prayers I was praying.

It's easy and religious to use prayer to ask God to change everything and then just go our merry way for the rest of the day. "God, please make the world better." "God, please make my marriage better." "God, please help my wife to treat me better." Then there's my personal favorite: "Change her (not me), oh God!"

The Lord showed me a much better way to pray those things. "God, please *use me* to make the world better." "God, please *use me* to make my marriage better." Even the prayer "Change *her,* oh God" soon became, "Change *me,* oh God."

Jesus never prayed one prayer that He wasn't willing to put his own life, action, and resource behind.

In Luke 23:34 Jesus says, "Father, forgive them, for they know not what they do."

Shortly after, Jesus would of course give His own life and shed His own blood for the remission and total forgiveness of the sins of all mankind. What a picture of putting action behind prayer!

Do you think Jesus ever went around saying, "Father, I'm going to get in my prayer closet now and pray the world figures out one day you really love them." No. He used those quiet prayer times to prepare His own heart and say, "Father, *use me* to show this world how much you love them."

Luke 5:15-17 says, "15 The news about Jesus spread all the more, so that crowds of people came to hear him and to be healed of their sicknesses. 16 But Jesus often withdrew to isolated places and prayed. 17 One day He was teaching... and the power of the Lord was present to heal..."

We see here that Jesus withdrew in prayer and to no surprise the power of the Lord was present to heal the next morning! He spent time in prayer hearing His Father's heart and plan, and then preparing Himself to be a partner in it.

I really believe that is what our Heavenly Father wants to do with us in this world. He desires to use us to demonstrate His love for humanity and to reveal His compassion for the hurting. We are truly His partners, as His power operates through our simple willingness and availability.

In John 3:16 Jesus says, "For God so loved the world that He gave His only begotten Son, that whosoever believes on Him would not perish but have everlasting life."

Jesus didn't just preach the message God so loved the world; He WAS the message God so loved the world! He lived it! He actually revealed the Father's love in His words, actions, attitudes, and teachings! He did not just pray prayers about how much God loved humanity and then hope the Father showed themm while He went on His merry way.

We try to make Christianity so complicated. Imagine praying "Father, USE me to bring peace to my home," instead of "Father help me bring peace to my home." When we pray "Father help me" our idea of what is supposed to happen and our ability to do it are at the center. When we pray "Father use me," our Heavenly Father's idea of what needs to happen and His ability to do it are at the center.

I can remember years ago me praying at a pastors meeting, "Father, bring in the lost to our churches! Bring them in oh God from the north, south, east and west; God, bring 'em in, bring 'em in!" It really sounded so spiritually sound and grounded.

Yet you know what the Father told me? He whispered, "Steve, I don't own a car." I thought about it for a little bit and realized He was right – we were the ones who had transportation! So I quickly changed my prayer to, "Father, use us to bring in those who don't know you. We'll bring 'em to church. They can ride with us."

This concept is so simple, be willing to be part of the answer to the prayers your Father leads you to pray.

Steve Eden

Chapter 8:
Secret Place Prayer

Psalm 91:1-2 says, "He who dwells in the <u>secret place</u> of the Most High shall abide under the shadow of the Almighty. 2 I will say of the Lord, "He is my refuge and my fortress; my God, in Him I will trust."

The culmination of all the Lord shared with me led to a practice I like to call "Secret Place Prayer." It is treating prayer as a place where I simply focus not on work to be done, but on being in the loving Presence of my Father.

<u>Jesus has taught me that prayer is not to be just one more Christian activity where we try to 'prove' our love for Him, but rather a place of rest, intimacy, security, honesty, and meditation on truth.</u> It is a place where we can spend quality time together-- similar to a husband and wife having a date night for the sole purpose of enjoying each other's company.

Isaiah 40:31 says, "But those who <u>wait</u> on the Lord shall renew their strength; they shall mount up with wings like eagles, they shall run and not be weary, they shall walk and not faint."

<u>The word "wait" here is not just sitting around waiting for the second coming of Jesus but actually means, "Braided together" and "To be intertwined."</u> It is literally like three chords wrapped so tightly they become one.

Truly we are renewed as Christians when we intertwine ourselves daily with Christ our Vine, our Source, and our Life – the One who not only gives us strength but who is our strength.

<u>Key Points In Secret Place Prayer:</u>

1) Learning To Rest

The reason there is so much burnout, frustration, and fatigue in the body of Christ today is there is little to no mention of rest.

Jeremiah 50:6 says, "My people have been lost sheep. Their shepherds have led them astray; They have turned them away on the

mountains. They have gone from mountain to hill; They have forgotten their resting place."

Led astray by shepherds because they weren't taught to work hard enough? To do more good deeds? To add more religious activity? No, led astray because they forgot their resting place. In order for us to run our race well, we need to understand we are as hard wired for receiving as we are for producing.

Because many pastors have struggled with rest and intimacy in prayer, many in their congregations have as well. In a recent survey, the majority of pastors said the only time they pray or read the Bible is to get a message for Sunday services. They cited little or no time to reflect or pause on how much their Heavenly Father loves them.

Because of this, many in the body of Christ have not had it modeled or taught that God loves them more than what they do for Him. They are unfamiliar with the reality that rest can be as maturing, valuable, and transforming as labor.

<u>The spirit of this age has programmed us for action and accomplishment with nary a wink at resting and receiving</u>. The world and even the church to some degree has said, "If you're not busy, you're not important." As Christians we must be careful that upon surrendering to Christ, we don't just trade our worldly busyness for Christian busyness.

God Rested, Why Not Us?

We need to take a cue from our Heavenly Father and learn to rest. There are many different types of prayer in the Bible: Intercession, praying our Fathers will into manifestation, petitioning God for needs, but we need times in prayer when we are not working but resting in our Father's arms.

Genesis 2:1-3 says, "1 Thus the heavens and the earth, and all the host of them, were finished. 2 And on the seventh day God ended His work which He had done, and He rested on the seventh day from all His work which He had done. 3 Then God blessed the seventh day and sanctified it, because in it He rested from all His work..."

If the God of the universe rested, we probably need times of rest as well. When you read the Genesis account, God didn't rest because He was tired from making too many galaxies. He rested simply to enjoy and reflect upon what He had made. So if we do not take time to rest and reflect, we can miss out on great opportunities to enjoy what our partnership with God has produced.

There is a time to be used of God towards His purposes in the Earth, but there's also a time to be stilled and be filled. There are times when prayer is used so things get changed, but there are times prayer is used so we get changed.

Psalm 46:10-11 says, "10 Be still, and know that I am God; I will be exalted among the nations, I will be exalted in the earth! 11 The Lord of hosts is with us; The God of Jacob is our refuge."

Resting in God lifts us out of thinking about what we don't have and helps us see how connected we are to the unlimited resources of Christ's Kingdom. That sounds so much better than prayer as excessive talking and promises to do better!

2) Jesus Is Personal

In Matthew 11:28-30 (The Message) Jesus says, "Are you tired? Worn out? Burned out on religion? <u>Come to Me. Get away with Me</u> and you'll recover your life. I'll show you how to take a real rest. Walk with me and work with me—watch how I do it. Learn the unforced rhythms of grace. I won't lay anything heavy or ill-fitting on you. Keep company with me and you'll learn to live freely and lightly."

Jesus didn't say, "Come to My doctrine," "Come to My teachings", or "Come to My philosophy" like most religious leaders. He said, "Come to Me!!" I believe this communicates and reveals His desire for us to have personal relationship and intimacy with Him over mere head knowledge.

In Christianity, if we miss a present tense, on-going, personal relationship with Jesus Christ, then I am afraid we have missed the whole thing. Even Jesus Himself said in John 5:39-40 that the purpose of the Scriptures is to bring us to Him.

Honestly, I do not believe in Jesus because of the Bible; I believe in the Bible because of Jesus. I do not believe in Jesus because of the miracles; I believe in miracles because of Jesus. His character and His Person have won my heart and empowered me to know He is who He says He is. It would have been more of a miracle to me had Jesus' incredible love and nature NOT produced any miracles! It's like – of course HE does miracles, how could someone with the richness of His constitution not do miracles?

Prayer needs to be a place where we can learn FROM Jesus-- not just about Him. Notice He says in Matthew 11 there is a yoke, but this yoke doesn't feel like weights; it feels like wings – empowering us to live "freely and lightly!"

3) Meditation On The Truth

Another aspect of secret place prayer is that it's a place to meditate on Truth. The word meditate means to, "think upon over and over; to ponder or reflect upon; to consider deeply."

Christian meditation is not the disengaging of the mind; that is new age and other religious hocus pocus. <u>Christian meditation is engaging the mind on Truth, on Jesus Christ, who He is, and who He says we are in Him.</u>

What God says about us is so hard to believe because the world has conditioned us to think so poorly of ourselves. <u>How is it possible that so many Christians who know what God says about them and have been taught His Word, can be completely undone by one bad word from someone else?</u>

It is probably because we do not take the time to think upon over and over again God's Truth. I know we get busy and distracted, but mind renewal is a huge component and weapon of the New Testament Christian.

Philippians 4:8 (New King James) says, "Finally, brethren, whatever things are true, whatever things are noble, whatever things are just, whatever things are pure, whatever things are lovely, whatever things are of good report, if there is any virtue and if

there is anything praiseworthy—<u>meditate on these things.</u>"

What is true? God's Word. What is pure? You are in Christ. What is lovely? Each day the Lord gives you.

There are many things in our lives, families, and careers which we can "consider deeply" and let occupy our minds, but in Philippians 4:8 Paul gives us a wonderful list! Here is the same passage in the Message Bible:

"Summing it all up, friends, I'd say you'll do best by <u>filling your minds and meditating</u> on things true, noble, reputable, authentic, compelling, gracious—the best, not the worst; the beautiful, not the ugly; things to praise, not things to curse."

This doesn't mean you don't see ugly things; it just means you don't allow yourself to meditate or dwell on them. It was once said, "You can't keep birds from flying over your head, but you *can* keep them from nesting in your hair."

Psalm 119:15-16 says, "I will <u>meditate</u> on Your precepts, and contemplate Your ways. 16 I will delight myself in Your statutes; I will not forget Your word."

As human beings we have the opportunity every day to choose life or death. Indeed, there are people who meditate day and night on death and negativity, and they aren't fun to be around.

Deuteronomy 30:19 says, "I have put life and death before you, blessing and cursing; therefore, choose life."

God makes it clear here in this passage that we have a choice. In secret place prayer, we want to make sure what we choose to 'consider deeply' each day lines up with God's Word and is life and blessing to us. Let's make sure it is Spirit and Truth.

Godly meditation brings death to every identity that is not from God, His Spirit, or His Word. Remember, if your view of you does not match God's view of you then you are wrong, not God.

Chapter 9:

Prayer, Problems, and Perspective

One of the most loving things our Father has ever done is NOT answer some of our prayers. I'm convinced that if He did we would most likely pray ourselves into immaturity. Imagine prayers such as, "God please fix all my problems," "God please don't give me any adversity," "Father please cause everyone to act right so I don't have to love unconditionally or forgive."

<u>Trials can be such wonderful opportunities to grow in Christ and learn to walk by the Spirit.</u> We love to declare to the Lord, "I pray when people see me, they see you." And yet the best chance to reveal the unconditional love and goodness of our Father's nature is when someone *isn't* supplying us the love to love them with! We then can utilize prayer to posture ourselves as a willing vessel for His

power to flow through to those who need Him.

When we experience trials at the hands of others, we often think it is because God needs to work on them; yet many times it may be because He is working on us. Imagine if our focus became what problems do FOR us instead of what they do to us.

Times of reflection and meditation in prayer allow us to ask questions such as, "Father why does that person rub me the wrong way?" "Father is there something in me that needs healed because I seem quick to anger and frustration?" You might have heard it said that "prayer changes things," but it's equally true that "prayer changes us" and can give us "Proper Problem Perspective."

Proper Problem Perspective

Whether you are in the midst of difficult trials, relationship frustrations, or demonic attack, it is very important that you first submit yourself to God before you respond to situations in the flesh, anger, or self pity.

These 7 problem perspectives can help!

1) God promises to work this for my good.

Romans 8:28 says, "And we know that in all things God works for the good of those who love him, who have been called according to his purpose."

Any situation may in the natural result in a "win" or a "loss," but for those of us in God's Kingdom, He has the power to make them all wins!! Even our failures become successes to God because He will never cease to grow us toward our highest good.

There is value to be mined like gold out of every life situation. Through many of my own trials, failures, and battles, I have learned invaluable things such as humility, dependence on God, and wisdom. I've even learned sin is sand in my machinery – it never works out for my good; never! Through mishandling my children I have learned the value of modeling apologies. Through difficulty in marriage, I have learned the value of selflessness, communication, and compromise.

2) God is going to use this to conform me to the image of His Son.

Romans 8:29 says, "For those God foreknew he also <u>predestined</u> to be conformed to the image of his Son, that he might be the firstborn among many brothers and sisters."

What joy to know that everything you go through can be used to make you more like Christ! Everything in life can be used to send you toward your destiny!

I have a friend who through a business deal gone bad had a strong urge to punch the other man. One day in prayer, the Lord said to my friend, "Where is your compassion for that gentleman and his obvious lack of relationship with Me?" My friend was immediately convicted and thanked the Lord for conforming Him to His image and changing His perspective! Remember when the sparks are flying around you that everything you are facing is sending you to your destiny!

3) God is using this to prepare me for the next level!

Romans 5:17 says, "For if, by the trespass of the one man, death reigned through that one man, <u>how much more will those who receive God's abundant provision of grace and of the gift of righteousness REIGN in life through the one man, Jesus Christ!</u>"

If you have never heard the term, "Training For Reigning," let me introduce it to you. God has predestined you and handcrafted you for reigning in this life. In Genesis 1:28 our instructions are: Be fruitful, multiply, replenish, and subdue. This goes hand in hand with Romans 5:17 above which says, "through God's grace and the free gift of Righteousness we reign in life." There are going to be times when you face problems and adversity simply because you are being prepared for bigger battles and subsequent victories ahead.

If someone wants to grow his physical muscles he must increase the resistance he pushes against incrementally. He cannot lift five pound dumbbells his whole life. In the same way, if we are to grow our faith muscles, there are times we must face increased resistance. The beauty is, we can know that when the enemy thought he was taking us down by opposing us, he was actually making us stronger and training us for reigning!

4) This is an invitation to the supernatural

In Matthew 5:43-45 Jesus says, "You have heard that it was said, 'Love your neighbor and hate your enemy.' ⁴⁴ But I tell you, love your enemies and pray for those who persecute you, ⁴⁵ that you may be children of your Father in heaven."

He goes on to say in verse 46 (paraphrase) "If you only love those who love you what is that to you? Even heathen do that."

Jesus is introducing the idea that we as Christians have another Source for our behavior and attitude than the behavior and attitude of others. We are actually able to demonstrate we have a Fountain in the Spirit that people of the world just do not have.

Anyone can have joy when all their situations, circumstances, relationships, and business deals

are perfect in the natural. Anyone can praise
God when all is well. Anyone can feel like
praying when all the calls are going our way.

Prayer and secret times with our Father help us
to realize when a spouse yells at us or mistreats
us, we now have an opportunity to abide in and
participate with God's Spirit! We can again
reveal we are supernaturally sourced! We will
never master the circumstances of our lives
until our hearts are mastered by Him.

5) God can use this to help others

**2 Corinthians 1:3-4 says, "Blessed *be* the
God and Father of our Lord Jesus Christ,
the Father of mercies and God of all
comfort, [4] who comforts us in all our
tribulation, that we may be able to comfort
those who are in any trouble, with the
comfort with which we ourselves are
comforted by God."**

There are so many times I have seen my pain
become other people's gain. I have gone
through tough situations where God has
comforted me and then used me to comfort
others who go through a similar situation.

I've heard it said, "Experience is the best teacher" but does it always have to be our personal experience? We can definitely learn from others missteps, reactions, and trials, and they can learn from ours. I know of a man who was an alcoholic for much of his young adult life. At around age 40 God delivered him and now he is a tremendous asset in God's hands to help deliver other young men who are bound by alcoholism.

6) I get to find out what is really in my heart

In Matthew 12:34 Jesus said, "For what is in the heart in abundance comes out of the mouth."

Humans are like grapes in that when they are squeezed, what is on the inside is going to come shooting out. If you are squeezed by difficulty and stress, or someone rubs you the wrong way; and anger, expletives, or a rabid dog come out, then the Lord uses that to address areas of your heart. He shows you where you need healing.

As I said before, even our failures can become successes to God if we allow Him to address them and don't hide them. Hiding them though is futile when you understand He sees everything anyway.

On the other hand, if you are squeezed in a situation of life, and love, joy, and peace come shooting out of you then it's time to get your praise on! You and the Lord both can celebrate your maturity, growth, and development in Him. Your prayers of "Father, when people see me I want them to see you" are coming to fruition.

When that does happen though, it is most likely because you have prepared your heart and mind on the front end of a situation. Unfortunately, many of us wait until we are confronted with a stressful circumstance and start praying, "Oh God, put a guard over my mouth and help me not say something terrible here!"

7) This reminds me to be thankful

1 Thessalonians 5:16-18 says, "Rejoice always, [17] pray without ceasing, [18] in everything give thanks; for this is the will of God in Christ Jesus for you."

You want to know what God's will is for your
life? How about giving thanks in all things.
What a weapon a thankful and grateful heart is
in prayer! Too often we go to God and tell Him
how big our problems are when we ought to be
telling our problems how big our God is!

Difficulties in the right perspective can really
make you thankful for what you do have or do
not have. For example, yes your spouse is
driving you crazy but at least you have one.
There are so many people out there who
struggle in finding a husband or a wife.

Maybe your child is noisy, doesn't always
mind, or is sometimes rebellious; but at least
you have children. There are many people out
there who do not or cannot have children.

Your job may not be optimum everyday; it may
even put you around people that bug you, but
guess what? There is a perspective within you
and can be brought about through prayer that
says, "Thank you Lord, that I have a job."

An ungrateful heart can make us susceptible to
the enemy in a big way. If we are not careful,
we can turn self-centered, even entitled; which

can diminish our countenance and attitude of gratitude. Our prayers can turn from intimacy, love, and freedom into a complete whining session.

Even in marriage, if our focus becomes on everything we DON'T like about our spouse, they can quickly diminish in value to us. What if instead we focus on what we like about them? They actually increase in value to us as our heart develops in thanksgiving to God.

Final Thoughts

In closing, I want to exhort you and let you know-- God loves you. He loves you because He's so good not because you're so good. He loves you because of who He is and not because of what you do. The truest thing about you will always be what God says about you.

Rest in His love. Embrace it, dance with it, live like it's yours; believe it and receive it. Rather than strive to be good, yield yourself to the good One. In all you do, live with your hands open before God; lay down your personal bill of rights. Embrace your need for His supply each and every day.

Do good works, but do them because you are saved not so you will be saved. Do them from your Father's love not for His love. Live in the grace your Heavenly Father has so amazingly provided you through Jesus Christ. He wants to be your daily supply and source.

Grow in your love for humanity through God's love for humanity, not through self effort. Live God centered and others minded knowing it is written, "He who waters others gets watered in the process." (Proverbs 11:25)

Be awakened to the prayerful practices of Humility, Intimacy, and Surrender. For these I believe are when we are most H-I-S!

H – Humility
I – Intimacy
S - Surrender

Reformations In Prayer

ABOUT THE AUTHOR

At the age of 20, Steve Eden had a personal encounter with Jesus Christ while attending Northeastern (OK) State University. Feeling burned out and like a complete failure as a young Christian, it was in that encounter Jesus told him, "Steve, I love you because of who I am not because of what you do. So I want you to live the rest of your life from My love and not for it."

From that time on, with the Holy Spirit's guidance, Steve has been on a journey to bring himself and others out of performance based Christianity and into a vibrant, present tense, intimate relationship with his Lord, Savior, Best Friend, and Sanctifier Jesus Christ.

Made in the USA
San Bernardino, CA
08 March 2016